CONTENTS

Drawing and Inking Tips

In the world of sword-and-sorcery, heroes can perform extraordinary feats of valour that would be impossible in the real world. However, it's still essential that your characters should look solid and believable. So here are some helpful hints to bear in mind.

1 First work out your hero's posture and attitude, using a wire frame. You can look in the mirror to establish how a pose might appear!

2 Build on your frame using basic shapes, such as cylinders and spheres. As you add them to your wire frame, you can start to see your figure taking shape. From here, draw a smooth outline around the shapes to flesh out your figure.

TOP TIP !

Most adult human figures are seven times the height of their head. Draw your character's head, then calculate his or her height by measuring three heads for the legs, one for the lower torso and two for the upper body.

HUMAN HEIGHT = 7 HEADS

3 When things are looking good, and your character is complete, you can start to ink the picture. Inking allows us to choose the best lines we have put down in pencil, and make them stand out from the rest.

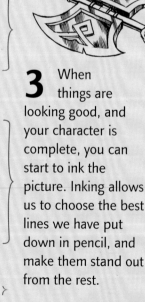

YOU CAN DRAW FANTASY FIGURES
DRAWING MAGICAL BEINGS

BY STEVE SIMS

Published in 2011 by Franklin Watts

Copyright © 2011 Arcturus Publishing Limited

Franklin Watts
338 Euston Road
London NW1 3BH

Franklin Watts Australia
Level 17/207 Kent Street
Sydney, NSW 2000

Artwork and text: Steve Sims
Editors: Kate Overy and Joe Harris
Designer: Steve Flight

Produced by Arcturus Publishing Limited,
26/27 Bickels Yard, 151–153 Bermondsey Street,
London SE1 3HA

A CIP catalogue record for this book is available from the British Library

Dewey Decimal Classification Number: 743.8'7

ISBN: 978 1 4451 0448 5

SL001641EN

Printed in Singapore

Franklin Watts is a division of Hachette Children's Books,
an Hachette Livre UK company.
www.hachettelivre.co.uk

Colouring Tips

1 After you finish inking, plan your colour scheme and then start laying down your base tones.

2 Next, colour the shaded areas using darker tones of the base colours. Note the shadows under this centaur's muscular arms and legs.

3 Finally, add some highlights to areas where light would reflect, using whites and lighter shades. Note how this brings a shine to the metal blade of his spear.

FOREST SPRITE

The forest sprites live among the moss and leaves of the woodland, barely visible to the untrained eye. They are not the biggest of creatures, yet they play a vital role in protecting the fairy queen's realm.

1 This little guy has long limbs and quirky features. Pay attention to the angular shape of the sprite's head when you start to plot your frame. Also draw the branch that he's perching on.

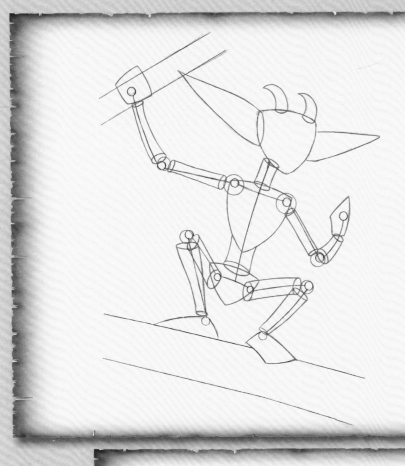

2 Build on your frame using basic shapes. Give the sprite large, bat-like ears and two small horns on the top of his head.

3 Sprites spend a lot of time in trees, so when you're fleshing him out, think about tree-dwelling creatures like monkeys, and the way that their limbs are formed. Start removing your construction shapes.

4 Once his body is in place, add the basic shape of two sets of wings. Give him an inquisitive expression and draw the magical ring he is holding. Large eyes and a small mouth will help to make him look otherworldly, as will his unusual hands and feet.

TOP TIP !

Studying trees where you live, or in photographs, will help you to recreate the branches and bark accurately.

5 Now add the final pencil details to your sprite. Give his furry patches some shading and draw the delicate veins on his wings and ears.

6 When inking your sprite, think about the areas that will be in shade, and add more black where his wings join his body. Make sure you keep the detail on the wings so that they look light and delicate.

FOREST SPRITE

7 As your sprite is a magical creature, you can really experiment with colour. Try giving him blue skin and use a mossy brown for his fur. Light, shimmering greens will work well for his wings, and bright yellow eyes will stand out against the blue face.

CENTAUR

Half man, half beast, the centaur has
the speed and power of a charging horse
coupled with the combat skills of a highly
trained warrior. Loyalty, wisdom and
superhuman strength make the centaur
an incredibly formidable opponent.

1 Start by drawing
your wire frame.
This figure is quite tricky,
so take the time to draw
the joints and limbs in
the correct position.
Getting the basic frame
right will get you off to a
good start.

2 Build on your frame using basic shapes. Pay special attention to the structure of the legs – horses have more leg joints than humans. It might be useful to use a picture of a horse as reference to help you get the right proportions.

3 Erase all the basic shapes once you have set out the outline of your figure. Mark in the main muscle sections on his chest. Add the outline of his flowing hair and tail. Draw the outline of his spear.

4 Start adding detail to your clean pencil drawing. Add his facial features, giving him a brave battle-ready expression. Draw in his armour and define his muscle tone. Add some tufts of fur to his hooves.

CENTAUR

TOP TIP!

Small lines and simple cross-hatching will create the impression of fur on the lower half of his body.

5 Now it's time to add all the final details. Give his armour interesting features, such as studs and chains. It's made of wood, so add some grainy lines too. Block out the shaded areas ready for inking.

6 Time to add your ink. Using solid areas of black on his bottom half will create depth and define the individual limbs. Stripes of ink on the hooves will make them look shiny.

7 The final step is to colour your centaur. Looking at different kinds of horses might inspire you to try some alternative colour schemes. Remember to match his hair colour and his tail colour.

ELF PRINCESS

The elf princess may appear young, but she is older and wiser than almost any other denizen of her world. She is gifted with the powers of ancient woodland magic and control over the forces of nature.

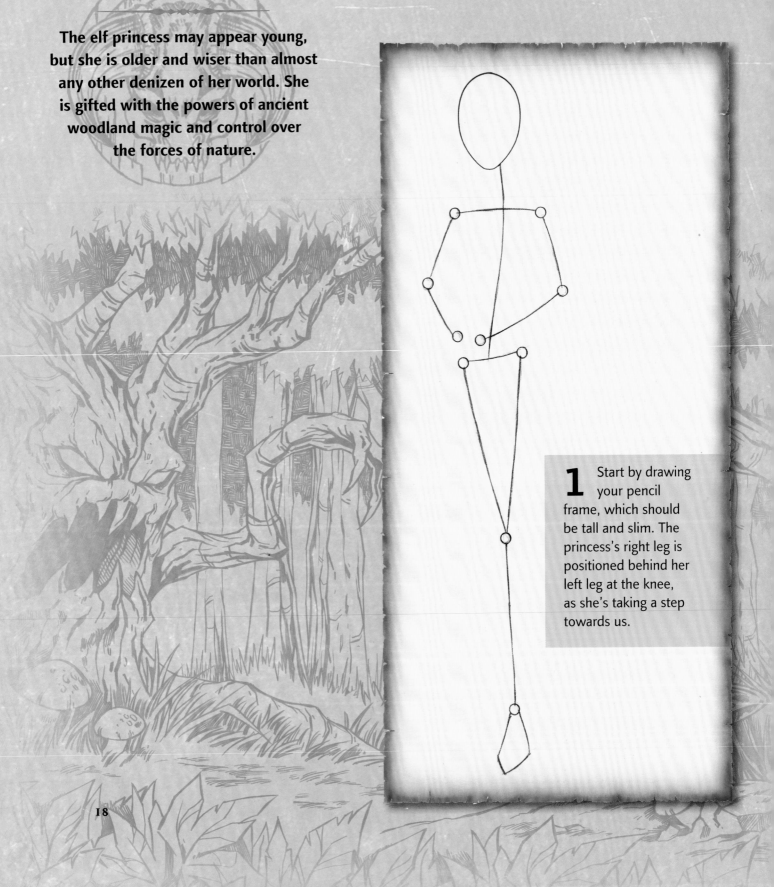

1 Start by drawing your pencil frame, which should be tall and slim. The princess's right leg is positioned behind her left leg at the knee, as she's taking a step towards us.

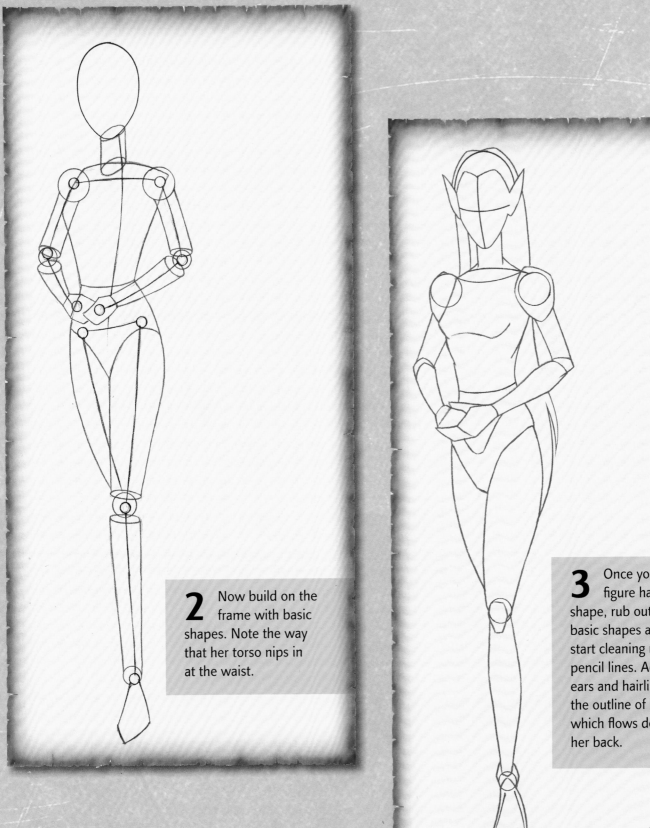

2 Now build on the frame with basic shapes. Note the way that her torso nips in at the waist.

3 Once your figure has taken shape, rub out your basic shapes and start cleaning up your pencil lines. Add the ears and hairline and the outline of her hair, which flows down her back.

4 Begin to flesh out your figure. Draw the fluid shape of her dress and belt and give her delicate, pretty facial features. Surround her with lots of butterflies.

TOP TIP !

If your character is moving, it will affect the clothing he or she is wearing. Mark on lines to indicate the direction in which the fabric is moving.

5 At the final pencil stage, add some embellishment to her dress and belt. Decorate her princess's tiara with precious stones. Mark in the light folds in her dress and the strands of her hair.

6 Now apply the ink making sure you keep your lines light and flowing. No heavy shading is needed for this delicate figure!

7 When colouring your elf princess, choose light, natural colours for her clothing. Use darker shades of the same colour to add areas of shading. Give her bright blonde hair and pale skin.

Creating a Scene

THE FOREST

You've finally mastered how to draw three different types of magical creatures, so now it's time to create a dramatic forest setting for them to live in. Imagine a mysterious and enchanted glade, complete with an abandoned well and fearsome living trees. It's like something out of a dream – or a nightmare!

1 Plot out the basic shapes of your forest scene. Eventually, we will need lots of trees in our forest. However at first it's best to concentrate on just one or two in the foreground, while you work out the overall shape and structure of your picture.

2 Now start to flesh out your main trees with branches. Note the way that the trunks split into broad boughs, which each divide into narrower branches. Sketch in the rough, jagged shapes for the leaves of the bush that sits in the foreground, and also draw the trunks of the trees that make up the background.

3 With our basic elements in place, we can now get stuck into pencilling our scene. Start thinking about textures, such as the gnarled trunks of the trees. Add more detail to the leaves in the canopy and in the foreground – these will frame the scene. Use short, choppy, upward strokes to draw blades of grass in lines across the page. These will break up the different levels of the forest floor.

4 Add areas of cross-hatching (dense, criss-cross lines) to the leaves that are in the shadow behind your main trees. Make the inside of the evil tree's mouth jet black. These techniques will add some depth to your image.

25

5 Now apply the ink. Use heavier strokes in the foreground to make objects feel nearby, and lighter lines in the background to make things feel more distant. Be careful not to go overboard with dark inking, or you'll start to lose the detail and texture from your image.

6 A forest image is bound to be largely green. So as to make your picture varied and interesting, you should use a variety of shades: blue-greens, yellow-greens, light and dark greens. Then add flashes of other, contrasting colours, like these vibrant pink and purple mushrooms.

Drawing Different Expressions

Changing a character's facial expression can make them look completely different. You can create an infinite number of different facial expressions simply by changing your character's eyes, eyebrows and mouth.

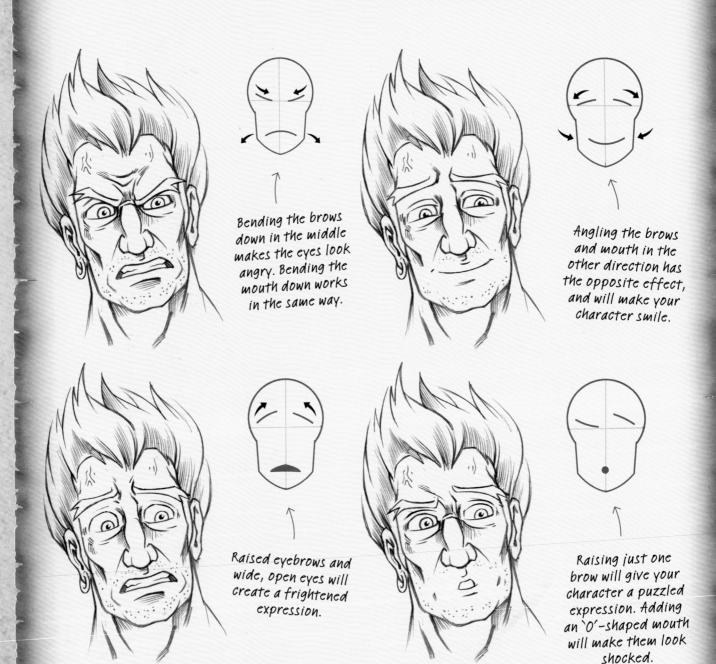

Bending the brows down in the middle makes the eyes look angry. Bending the mouth down works in the same way.

Angling the brows and mouth in the other direction has the opposite effect, and will make your character smile.

Raised eyebrows and wide, open eyes will create a frightened expression.

Raising just one brow will give your character a puzzled expression. Adding an `O`-shaped mouth will make them look shocked.

Expressions Gallery

Try some of these expressions with the many characters you create.

A knowing smile and narrowed eyes show cunning.

A furrowed brow and a yelling mouth will indicate rage.

Pursed lips and scowling eyes will make your character look menacing.

Raised eyebrows and a gaping mouth will show shock or surprise.

TOP TIP !

Use these tips as a basis for your own experiments with expressions. If you get stuck, grab a mirror and start pulling different faces. It's a great way to learn how the face works. Just make sure you don't scare yourself!

Play around with expressions, but remember your character's personality. A happy face on a bad-tempered beast will just look wrong!

Glossary

boughs the thickest branches of a tree
cross-hatching a way of shading using lines going
  in two or more different directions
denizen someone who lives in a particular place
embellishment a decoration intended to make
  something more attractive
furrowed with deep lines or wrinkles
gnarled twisted and rough because of age
highlights the lightest coloured parts of an image
posture the position of someone's body
proportions the size of different things compared
  to each other
shimmer shine with a gentle, flickering light
texture the way the surface of an object looks
  or feels
tiara a band worn on the head, often made of a
  precious metal and studded with jewels
torso the middle part of your body, from which
  the limbs and head extend
tufts bunches joined together at one end
valour courage in battle

Further Reading

Drawing and Painting Fantasy Worlds by Finlay
  Cowan (Impact Books, 2006)
Fantasy Drawing Workshop by John Howe
  (Impact Books, 2009)
How to Draw Wizards, Warriors, Orcs and Elves by
  Steve Beaumont (Arcturus Publishing, 2006)

Index